Donald Trump

American

Donald Trump American

John Q. Public

Ars Americana Press

Published in the United States of America by Ars Americana Press.

Contents

Introduction

This book is meant to be a small counterbalance to the 95% negative coverage the mainstream media gives to president Donald Trump. I want to highlight some positive things about him and his accomplishments. Just so you know where I am coming from, I'm a working class American. A white male raised in a home of political Democrats and politically independent myself. The following is my perspective and opinion, you can take it or leave it as you wish.

"Every day I wake up determined to deliver a better life for the people all across America that have been ignored, neglected and abandoned".

~Donald Trump

Chapter One

During the 2016 election, I was unimpressed with the candidates put forward by both parties. This was nothing new itself. But this time it looked particularly bleak. By the time it boiled down to Donald Trump and Hillary Clinton I was faced with the king of real estate developers and a treasonous criminal. "Is this the best we as a nation can come up with"? I thought to myself. "Surely we can do better than this". But these were to be our choices. There was, however, no choice in my mind who was the one to support. I couldn't possibly support Clinton. So it had to be Trump. While I do wish people would understand that we don't actually have an official two party system, and that they can and should feel free to vote outside of Republicans and Democrats, in this case the other candidates were no better. So Trump it was. As I was resigned to this situation I began to think about it. I didn't really know much about Trump in all fairness. I've never met him. Maybe he will be better than I assume he will. I should give him a chance.

I wasn't impressed with Obama at all. And Bush Jr. could certainly have done a better job than he did. Bill Clinton was just as bad as Bush Jr. and Obama. Of course the less said about Bush Sr. the better. 28 years of incompetence, scandal, and lies. Trump couldn't possibly do any worse than these 4 guys. Let's see what he does if he wins. Now of course the bar was set pretty low by his predecessors but this was where we were.

It was interesting to watch the election process. Everyone hated him and attacked ruthlessly. I'd never seen anything like the attacks he suffered (and still suffers), just like I'd never seen anyone keep going in the face of such hostility. But nothing stopped him. Just like during the primary. The man was bulletproof. I did enjoy how he seemed to piss everybody off. Especially the media, both political parties, and the elite. Even if he lost it would be a good show. Very entertaining.

But Donald Trump continued to move ahead and surprised a lot of people by winning the election. I was relieved that Hillary Clinton didn't win but now had to wait and see how Donald Trump would perform as President. Could a real estate developer surprise me? I was skeptical to say the least. But, as his administration began to unfold, It appeared that maybe he was going to impress me after all. It's unfortunate how polarized the country has become since then. People either love Trump or hate him, by and large. But that same polarization has spread into many other areas of life.

Unlike many presidents before him, Donald Trump actually kept his word and began to work for the American people. Especially the working class stiff who feels like the country is letting him/her down. The people in the states that nobody seems to care about. Or those who have seen prosperity and prospects dwindle while the wealthy and privileged receive more and more. These people didn't want handouts, more government, and more social programs. They wanted a chance to work and make a life for, and by themselves. These are the people that elected Donald Trump to the presidency.

People had said that Trump wasn't a Washington insider. Because of that and his private fortune, he wouldn't be a slave to the special interest groups. I hoped this would turn out to be correct. I have seen the money and power of Capitol Hill corrupt people before. But the people turned out to be right. The special interests and the deep state have no hold on him. But he still faces an uphill battle. Half his own political party, the Democrats, the media, the elite, and a large portion of the population are against him, and he has arguably the hardest, most stressful job in the world. It's hard to do anything under those circumstances.

So as I began to realize that he was doing a pretty good job all things considered, I said to myself, "Well, I figured he couldn't be any worse than his 4 predecessors", and not only was I right, he is actually doing pretty good.

I had been busy with my life, and I almost allowed others to dictate what I think. I don't like politics and usually stay out of politics discussions so I didn't want to think much about it.

But, Donald Trump can't get a fair shake from the

mainstream media. They stopped being objective or even journalists a while ago. Now they only exist to push agendas and narratives. They are propaganda peddlers. The American version of Pravda. So now let's look at some of his accomplishments, and then his character in contrast to the demonization he continually suffers at the hands his enemies.

"Let me list to you some of the things that we've done in just a short period of time. Again, each of these actions is a promise I made to the American people. We've withdrawn from the job-killing disaster known as Trans-Pacific Partnership. We're going to make trade deals, but we're going to have one-on-one deals, bilateral. We are now in the process of beginning to build a promised wall on the southern border. We've begun preparing to repeal and replace Obamacare."

~Donald Trump

Chapter Two

President Trump has actually accomplished quite a bit in 4 years. But most people have probably never heard of most of it since the media won't report anything positive about him. All they do is attempt to make him look as bad as they can. So here is just a sample of what he has done. There is a lot more. At the end of the book there will be links to where you can get a more in depth idea of what he has done for Americans. They are among the sources I used.

So the President has signed 3 bills providing help or justice for native American tribes. One compensated the Spokane tribe for lands that they lost in the mid 20th century. Another officially recognizes the Little Shell tribe of the Chippewa, while the third provides for native language programs. I don't know how often other administrations did things for native Americans, but this seems pretty good.

Crime is an area where Trump can claim a victory for his presidency. Violent crime has fallen each year he has been in office. During the last 2 years before his election, violent crime rose each year.

More bills that president Trump has signed include the FOSTA act, a broad bill that gives many new tools to law enforcement and victims in the fight against sex trafficking, as well as a bill legalizing industrial hemp. And people have been fighting to get hemp decriminalized forever as there is no good reason for it to be prohibited.

Even his fiercest enemies can't downplay his contribution to the fight against sex trafficking.

Through his efforts of diplomacy, the presidents actions have freed a dozen hostages from their captors and that includes hostages that president Obama failed to free. You'll never hear that on the news.

Trump also directed the secretary of education to end one of the most disturbing, disastrous, and damaging influences that American education has ever been cursed with. One that has brought tears of frustration to student and parent alike. Common Core education standards.

Terminally ill patients can now try experimental treatments that were previously not allowed thanks to Right To Try legislation that Trump signed.

This is one of my personal favorites. Those who abuse animals now face tougher punishment since the president signed legislation making animal cruelty a federal felony.

Airports must now provide space for breastfeeding mothers because of legislation signed by Donald Trump.

Donald Trump appointed 5 openly gay ambassadors and empowered the openly gay ambassador to Germany to spearhead a global initiative that would work to decriminalize homosexuality worldwide.

Over 400,000 manufacturing jobs have been created during the Trump administration.

The president has also used his negotiating skills to broker a peace deal that has gotten both Bahrain and the United Arab Emirates to normalize their relations with Israel. Something nearly anyone would have considered impossible before. And not long after that he got Kosovo, a country with a Muslim majority, and Serbia, a country with a Christian majority, to agree to economic cooperation after a history of violence and failed negotiations. Both countries will also open embassies in Jerusalem, thereby recognizing Jerusalem as the capitol of Israel. In addition, Kosovo will officially recognize Israel as a nation.

But not content to stop there, Trump has developed a foreign policy he calls the "Trump Doctrine". Its philosophy is to stop Americas involvement in endless wars abroad. Wars that lead to thousands of dead Americans and foreigners, destruction, debt, and ill will, all with no benefit to anyone. Trump seeks to end all of this, thankfully. And not only that, but he has been nominated THREE TIMES for the Nobel prize for peace. These actions genuinely deserve such a nomination. He was also previously nominated for his efforts to achieve peace and reconciliation between North and South Korea. Not bad for a guy considered by his opponents to be confrontational and a bully. These achievements are something almost no other president has managed to accomplish. Certainly none of the previous 4 presidents did anything comparable.

Back at home, president Trump signed the First Step Act. This is major criminal justice reform. Among its provisions, the act lowers the sentence for 3rd strike drug convictions from life to 25 years as well as other reduced sentencing, some of which is retroactive. Black Americans are 90% of those benefiting from these retroactive reductions.

Another benefit to black Americans, Trump gave a 14% increase in funding to historically black universities and colleges. And yet people are calling our president a racist.

The domestic economic policies of president Trump are responsible for many historic milestones. Poverty in general fell to 11.8% under his administration, a 17 year low. Poverty for Hispanic and black Americans reached the lowest point ever since the data has been recorded. His policies have also created the following effects. The stock market soared to heights never before seen, and the same for median household income. Black, Hispanic, and Asian

American unemployment reached the lowest levels EVER RECORDED. Youth unemployment has reached a 50 year low and Women's unemployment hit a 65 year low.
This was all before the economic downturn of the COVID-19 lockdown, which was not Trumps fault. The economy is actually doing quite well in spite of that.

Does this sound like something the worst president in history could accomplish? Donald Trump has done things that few any presidents have done. And he has done it with the Democrats, some Republicans, the media, Hollywood, Academia, and many Americans attacking him every chance they get. How well would you do your job under those conditions?

This is a partial list of what he has done, but it gives you a very different idea of his administration that you would get from the mainstream media or social media. It shows solid, genuine, meaningful works in both the foreign and domestic arenas. All Americans, including minorities, are benefitting from this presidents efforts.

"Well, first of all never think of yourself as average. You started off with the wrong question because you are not average".

~Donald Trumps response to a woman asking him how an average person like her can begin.

Chapter Three

President Donald Trump is routinely vilified by the press and social media. They only report on him in a negative light. They will spin anything they can and take quotes and actions out of context in order to create a negative image of him. They will cherry pick data and outright lie. It really is disgusting the lows to which they will sink. You can't even call it journalism. It truly is propaganda.

He is a threat to special interest groups that have purchased Washington D.C. and a threat to the deep state. They will do or say anything to try to turn the American people against him. The media attacks him 24/7. They are relentless. And as we approach the 2020 election it only gets crazier and more intense. But how about a look at

Trump from a different and more honest perspective. Some of the not so well known stories about this man. A more truthful look into his nature.

You may have heard about this but it is a good story. Donald Trump was going to a Paula Abdul concert in 1991 with girlfriend Marla Maples when he observed a guy beating another guy with a baseball bat. Trump ordered his driver to pull over and Trump exited the limo and yelled at the attacker to stop. Witnesses observed this and told reporters about it at the time. Marla Maples was seen tugging at his arm telling him to stop. The guy spoke with Trump briefly and then fled the scene. Now the interesting thing about this is that later, when interviewed by James Rosen, Trump was unwilling to say much about it. He had to have the story dragged out of him. He told Rosen; "I'm not looking to play this thing up, I'm surprised you found out about it." This is not the egotistical loudmouth that the Media portrays Trump as. If Trump was the man they say he is he would be bragging this story up and talking about it. Even when campaigning Trump didn't talk about this despite how it would benefit him. It says something about his character.

In his days as a real estate developer in new York, Trump was known by people in the black community as someone you could go to for a business loan when the bank wouldn't give you a loan, which was a common experience for black people. Trump would give you a loan for your business personally. One time he was approached by a man who had taken a loan, the man had a check for Donald to repay the loan. Donald asked him if this was the check. The guy said yes. Donald ripped it up and said "Go run your business". This is from an interview with a man involved in the incident. A link to the interview can be found in the appendix of this book. This is not the image we get of the president. This is not the behavior of a self serving egotistical maniac. Nor is this the behavior of a racist.

On a similar note, Donald Trumps Palm Beach country club was the first to allow black people in. Again, is this the action of a racist? And along with Muhammad Ali and Rosa Parks, Trump was awarded the Ellis Island Medal of Honor, which is an award for Patriotism, Diversity, brotherhood, and tolerance. Yep, Trumps sounds pretty racist to me. But seriously, many Americans are absolutely convinced that is exactly what he is.

Trump is said to be an associate of Jeffrey Epstein, yet Trump famously banned Epstein from Mar-a-Logo after Epstein hit on the teenage daughter of a club member. A pedophile who is a friend and associate of Epstein wouldn't act in this fashion. These people cover for each other and their collective vile practices. While others are covering for Epstein, Trump is not.

There was a U.S. Marine sergeant who was wrongfully imprisoned in Mexico in 20014 for seven months. After getting out and coming home, Donald Trump gave him a check for $25,000 to help him out after his ordeal and to thank him for his service. I doubt that this is the behavior of a man who despises military veterans, and yet the media paints Trump as a president that disrespects our troops.

How about the time that a young boy with a rare breathing illness needed to get across the country to get medical treatment, but the airlines wouldn't fly him because of all the medical equipment needed to keep him alive. The boys parents contacted Donald Trump and told him of their problem. Trump flew the boy, his parents, and 3 nurses from L.A. to New York on Trump Force One, his private Boeing 727.

There was a segment on Oprah back in 2011 showing Trump spending some time in the shoes of his employees at his hotel. He was the Bellman, a waiter, and part of the cleaning staff (video linked in the appendix). Most people in his position wouldn't do that even as a one off for a tv show.

In 1986, a farmer in Georgia had a bank debt of $300,000. He would lose the family farm if he couldn't pay. He took out a life insurance policy on himself. He then committed suicide so his family could keep the farm, but he didn't pay attention to the clause in the policy that voided payment for suicide. The story made the news and eventually Donald Trump heard of it. He convinced the bank to give them an extension and also helped pay the debt. 30 years later, the daughter of the dead farmer spoke up at a Trump presidential rally and told the crowd of Trumps generosity and his appreciation of farmers and common Americans.

When hurricane Sandy struck the United States East coast in 2012, Trump let hundreds of evacuees stay in the atrium of Trump tower, giving coffee and food.

I know this isn't much compared to all the negativity spewed by the media, but I am only one guy. Still, this should give you something to show people who may be on the fence about the president. Trump haters will probably not be convinced, but this book might sway some folks view of Him.

I had never heard of any of these stories when Trump announced his candidacy in 2016. I thought he was a typical real estate developer, a profession I don't have a high opinion of. I work in the trades and have seen many of these people. But after reading these stories and looking at his performance during the last 4 years, I have come to believe that he is a better person than I gave him credit for. And I came to that conclusion myself. I didn't just mindlessly absorb what others had said about him, good or bad.
It's easy to just think what the media tells you to. We are all busy and it is quicker and easier to just let somebody else tell us what to think than to engage in critical thinking ourselves. But that makes it easy for others to control us, and we don't even realize what has happened. I believe

that is what is going on in America with the medias Trump
coverage. People are being controlled but they don't see it.

21

Chapter Four

The media is always downplaying the popularity of the President. Fake news stories about his campaign being in trouble, or trailing Joe Biden in the polls. I thought I would take a more fair look at some of that as well.

At a joint Biden-Harris appearance (the first joint appearance of the ticket I think) in Arizona, nobody showed up at all. All 45 people on site were either the Biden-Harris team or the press. No American citizens showed up at all. Pretty telling for a big event like that. Meanwhile, right around the same time, there was a rally for Donald Trump in BEVERLY HILLS CALIFORNIA! Hundreds of people marched down Rodeo drive. Signs proclaiming support for Trump from Jews, Latinos,

Chinese, and LGBT groups were seen prominently. Kind of an ominous sign if you ask me.

Biden spoke to a 30 car rally in Ohio in mid October. A rally that had little energy and was attended by Trump supporters chanting 4 more years. But also in mid October, there was a 30,000 car rally in Florida by Latinos for Trump. And in late September there were hundreds of cars in a rolling rally for Trump in the traditionally blue state of Hawaii. But the media keeps telling us that Joe Biden is ahead of Trump in the polls. Does anybody else see a disconnect between these rallies and the polls?

On September 9th 2020 there were a literal handful of people at a Biden Rally in Michigan, all separated by social distancing circles. A pretty sad turnout for the guy ahead of Trump in the polls. But the very next day in Michigan on September 10th, there was a packed event for Donald Trump. Thousands of people gathered in support of the president. On the next page are photos from the events. Biden's event on the top of the page, Trumps event on the bottom of the page.

There are many more examples like these, but you get my point. Donald Trump is plainly a lot more popular than the media would like us to think. People need to use their own eyes and think for themselves. Looks around. Donald Trump has a lot of support nationwide and he wouldn't have that if he was incompetent or corrupt like the left and their media allies say he is. I myself am more firmly in support of Donald Trump than I was 4 years ago. And I am basing this on what I see going on in out country, not what some news outlet or talking head is telling me. I think for myself.

Please look at the links in the appendix to get more information and verify things for yourself. All credit goes to the respective sources. Especially the videos. You will discover things you didn't know about the man and you will support and respect him even more.

If you like Donald Trump, I hope you enjoyed this and have an even greater respect for him. If you don't like him, I hope you can set aside your opinions for a short time and give some thought to what you have read here.

"Together, We will make America strong again. We will make wealthy again. We will make America proud again. We will make America safe again. And yes, together, we will make America great again. Thank you. God bless you. And God bless America".

~Donald Trump

Appendix

Information for this book came from the following sources, and all respective credit goes to them.

https://frankreport.com/2020/04/18/one-hundred-twenty-five-amazing-accomplishments-of-president-donald-j-trump/

www.bbc.com

https://nypost.com/2020/09/29/donald-trump-gets-third-nomination-for-nobel-peace-prize/

https://www.foxnews.com/politics/trump-second-nomination-for-nobel-peace-prize

https://www.foxnews.com/politics/what-is-first-step-act-5-things-to-know-about-the-criminal-justice-reform-law

www.pjmedia.com

https://thepoliticalinsider.com/trump-rescues-child/

https://www.theepochtimes.com/donald-trump-apparently-stopped-a-mugging-in-1991-resurfaced-report-says_2031210.html

https://youtu.be/wK1ylcdMukQ

https://visiontimes.com/2016/11/15/untold-stories-of-donald-trump.html

https://www.pacificpundit.com/2020/09/10/trump-campaign-rally-vs-biden-in-michigan/

https://nypost.com/2020/10/12/biden-speaks-to-30-cars-of-supporters-at-ohio-drive-in-rally/

https://www.worldtribune.com/latinos-for-trump-caravan-in-florida-had-30000-cars-nobody-shows-for-biden-rally-in-arizona/

29